Praise for *The Two Pillars of Reco*

"Addiction is a complex condition best addressed with a holistic approach attending biological, psychological, social, and spiritual needs. Dr. Kane manages to distill this into a framework of Brain and Behavior. The Two Pillars of Recovery is a simple but profound way for people with addiction to better understand and manage their condition and their lives."

~ **Kelly J. Clark, MD, MBA, DFASAM**
President, American Society of Addiction Medicine
Former Chief Medical Officer, CleanSlate Centers
Founder, Addiction Crisis Solutions

"A must read for our patients entering treatment for their addiction disease. Clearly the workbook points out it is the patient's responsibility and commitment to make change, and explains why they feel as they do. The workbook gives them a clear pathway to recovery."

~ **Mark L. Kraus, MD, DFASAM**
Assistant Clinical Professor of Medicine, Yale School of Medicine
Past Vice President, American Society of Addiction Medicine
Chief Medical Officer, Connecticut Counseling Center

"This is a useful and practical guide for those who are looking for a traditional approach to recovery from addictions. Dr. Kane presents information and strategies in a straightforward yet knowledgeable way that will be refreshing to those struggling to make sense of their lives."

~ **Theresa B. Moyers, PhD**
Department of Psychology, University of New Mexico

"Dr. Geoff Kane's Recovery Workbook is testament to an effective educational approach: Keeping it simple makes the message even more powerful."

~ **David C. Lewis, MD**
Professor Emeritus of Medicine and Community Health and the
Donald G. Millar Distinguished Professor of Alcohol and Addiction
Studies, Brown University

Act now, before things get worse.

The Two Pillars of Recovery® Workbook

What People with Addiction Need to Know and Do for Lasting Sobriety

Second Edition

Geoff Kane, MD, MPH

A MEETINGHOUSE SOLUTIONS PUBLICATION

Material in this booklet first appeared in
NCADD Addiction Medicine Updates
on ncadd.org, the website of
the National Council on Alcoholism
and Drug Dependence.

First Edition
© 2014 by Geoffrey P. Kane, MD, MPH

Second Edition
© 2019 by Geoffrey P. Kane, MD, MPH and Meetinghouse Solutions, LLC

ALL RIGHTS RESERVED

ISBN: 978-0-9991139-0-5

Contents

Author's Note iv

Foreword by Andrea G. Barthwell, MD v

1. Introduction 1
2. The Two Pillars of Recovery® 2
3. *Keep Your Distance!* 4
4. *Ask for Help!* 6
5. Falling Dominoes: Or, Why You Can't Have "Just One" 8
6. Sedative-Hypnotic Medications: Nothing to be Relaxed About 10
7. Recovery: Can You Have It *Your* Way? 13
8. It All Comes Down to Your Choices 15
9. My Commitments: Workbook and Recovery Journal 17

Author's Note

During my forty-plus years of helping people understand and cope with addiction, several thousand individuals seeking recovery have shared their stories with me. Their successes and mistakes have taught me what is most important.

Their collective experience revealed that individuals in active addiction who wish to move into recovery are wise to adopt two actions: Consistently avoid addictive substances and persistently seek help from others. The rationale behind the two actions is explained in this booklet in terms of brain science as well as practical experience because it turns out that brain science supports the same conclusions.

If you are tired of being stuck in active addiction, have hope. Let this booklet guide you to take responsibility for *keeping your distance* and *asking for help*.

Geoff Kane
Brattleboro, Vermont

Disclaimer

This booklet is intended to provide information, even inspiration, to the public. It is not treatment and should not be used in place of individualized professional care. I've quoted "The treatment of addiction is people" since 1974 and consider it true to this day. If you are stuck in addiction, I hope you find professionals and peers with whom to cultivate trust and honesty.

Acknowledgments

The author is indebted to editors Jeffrey Kelliher and Ann Landenberger, and to Ben Briggs, Leah Brock, Amelia Darrow, David Kane, Bahman Mahdavi, Teresa Pettinato, Grady Smith, and Stephen Wilcox, all of whom made this publication possible.

Photo Credits

Cover and page 2: istock.com/ssuni; page 4: istock.com/Timotale; page 6: istock.com/kieferpix; page 8: istock.com/Jayne_Louise; page 10: istock.com/WoodysPhotos; page 13: istock.com/oatawa; page 15: istock.com/denisik11; back cover: Jeff Woodward.

Foreword

The Two Pillars of Recovery® Workbook: What People with Addiction Need to Know and Do for Lasting Sobriety is a real triumph and an important resource—especially for individuals who realize they are addicted to alcohol or another drug but are stuck, unable to achieve a full life in recovery.

Geoff Kane, MD, MPH has provided addiction medicine professionals, therapists, and others involved in the addiction treatment world with a well-written volume of essays that explain the brain disease with clarity, conviction, and the kind of brilliance that takes difficult concepts and turns them into clear, plain language. Not only does Kane examine the disease and the two most common causes of failure to build on gains made in treatment and repeated relapses, he also shows the reader how to change. Anyone finding themselves estranged from their own lives and the lives of others due to alcoholism or another addiction will treasure the reflective, observant, and introspective qualities of this booklet's self-analysis and journal section as it will show them how to be who they want to become.

Dr. Kane's long career and his success in helping individuals addicted to alcohol and other substances to recover shows in the essays and in the self-analysis section. This little jewel closes the gap between academic journals, which are out of reach for anyone other than clinical and academic researchers, and commercial self-psychology books, which are targeted at individuals who need to acknowledge that they have the disease. The field is full of commercially-prepared workbooks used in treatment that follow the 12 Steps and the days of 28-day programs. What has not been available is a guidebook to answer the paralyzing triad of **guilt**—in response to doing something wrong, **shame**—being something wrong with an eroded sense of self, and **suffering**—the absence of pleasure and happiness. Treatment professionals and addictionists know that this triad derails all but the most deeply engaged—the persons who are willing to suspend other aspects of their lives in service of their recovery.

Until now we have not had anything to give individuals in need of such engagement, perhaps following an intervention or a treatment episode, to stimulate practical thinking and help them set priorities to protect their recovery. Kane recognizes that unless and until they answer the question, "What do I do now?" those individuals will be lost.

Two simple tenets are taught: *Keep Your Distance*, which nurtures responsibility to minimize the risk of resuming substance use, and *Ask for Help*, which nurtures actions to overcome shame and build resilience. These tenets are the basis of the included Workbook and Recovery Journal (My Commitments), which together help create insight into the true nature and extent of one's disease and provide a roadmap to overcoming plateaus in recovery. If you are a treatment professional, you owe it to your patients to read this tiny powerhouse of information and motivation. If you are estranged from yourself or others because of an addiction, you can do no better than to read and work this book with its approachable and person-friendly text that will help you forgive, accept, and heal.

Andrea G. Barthwell, MD, DFASAM
Chief Medical Officer, Treatment Management Company, LLC
Founder and Director, Two Dreams Outer Banks
President, Encounter Medical Group, PC
Past President, American Society of Addiction Medicine
Deputy Director, Office of National Drug Control Policy (2002-2004)

1. Introduction

Are you stuck in active addiction? If you answered "Yes," I'll bet you hurt. And the reality is that unless you commit to recovery and take appropriate action, the painful consequences of your addiction will likely grow. Don't stay stuck so long that your suffering and the suffering of those who care about you become unbearable.

I've witnessed extremes of suffering that might have been avoided if those involved had acted sooner. I sat with a father whose liver had failed from years of drinking alcohol as he worried about what would become of his family when he died. On the day she lost parental rights to her child, I sat with a mother who had repeatedly returned to use of heroin and cocaine. I sat with a man who had shared needles after telling him of his infection with the Human Immunodeficiency Virus (HIV). I sat with a spouse deciding to end a marriage not for lack of love, but because staying so close to the addicted partner was intolerable.

Ambivalence about change is normal. You might complain that "Recovery means change, and change is scary and hard." I might agree, and then point out that change becomes easier as soon as we accept the facts and begin. Besides, don't you have a strong incentive to change? There's more you can lose. And science reassures us we are built to change—our brains adjust and adapt as long as we live. The biggest obstacles to moving from addiction to recovery are often false pride (stubbornness, independence, ego) and the faulty logic of addiction that rates the urge for more drug above protecting personal safety, family, and community.

Stop collecting painful consequences. Establish safety, balance, and satisfaction in your life. This booklet can help guide you from active addiction into lasting recovery. Know, however, that commitment and action are required. Addiction is a human and biological process that occurs in nature. So is recovery. Nature operates through cause and effect. Your results will depend on what you do and don't do, not on your talent or good intentions.

You will be more likely to succeed in recovery if you understand the laws of nature that govern addiction and recovery from addiction, and if you adopt the two key actions that work with those laws of nature to allow recovery to happen. Sections 2 through 8 in this booklet are drawn from articles I wrote for the website of the National Council on Alcoholism and Drug Dependence (www.ncadd.org) as NCADD Addiction Medicine Updates. The articles describe these two key recovery actions and support their use based on both practical wisdom—the successes and mistakes of individuals with addiction who have gone before you—and the latest brain science.

The most important sections of this booklet, however, are the Workbook and Journal pages that follow the educational material. What I have written is far less important than the commitments *you* write—as you step away from active addiction and into healthy relationships.

Active addiction is an example of negative spirituality: It destroys relationships. Recovery is an example of positive spirituality: It builds and restores relationships. Embrace recovery and you will enrich your life with the rewards that flow from positive spirituality, including deeper connections, meaning, and purpose—and more abundant love and humor.

2. The Two Pillars of Recovery®

In the United States, an estimated 20 million people have problems with alcohol and/or other drugs. Many of these individuals attempt to get sober, but remain stuck using addictive substances because they try to fix things their own way—and berate themselves when nothing changes—unaware they are working *against* the laws of nature. Much like drivers who hit the gas but go nowhere when their car is stuck in snow, they keep using alcohol and other drugs because they don't understand why they are stuck or how to work *with* the laws of nature—laws that govern human behavior, addiction, and recovery from addiction—to cope with their problems.

Behavior is everything we can observe an organism do. Examples of human behavior include talking, eating, driving, dancing, breathing, and even body language that reveals emotions the person has not recognized.

Human behavior originates in the central nervous system, which consists of the brain and spinal cord. The brain is made up of the cerebrum (its outermost layer is the wrinkled cerebral cortex that we picture when we think "brain"), the brain stem, and the cerebellum. Portions of the brain stem and the inner layer of the cerebrum work together as the limbic system.

Laws of nature are often understood through science. The science of the nervous system is called neurobiology. A basic principle of the **neurobiology of behavior** is that *lower centers of the central nervous system can, and routinely do, act independently of higher centers.* For instance, the knee jerk reflex (a behavior) utilizes only a small segment of the lower end of the spinal cord. Breathing is driven by a nerve center in the lower brain stem.

The cerebral cortex, which supports conscious thought, is not routinely involved in reflexes or in breathing. We can involve the cortex if we tense our leg muscles or hold our breath, but that merely interrupts the automatic behaviors. It does not make them go away.

Instinctual behaviors such as eating (gratifies and protects the individual) and sex (gratifies the individual and protects the species) are more complicated than knee jerks and breathing. They are driven by the upper brain stem and the limbic system.

Instinctual behaviors can proceed without conscious thought and, at times, proceed *despite a conscious decision not to engage in them.* For example, have you ever eaten a second helping or a dessert right after you decided that you'd be better off without it? In experimental animals, if scientists alter a specific area in the region of the upper brain stem called the hypothalamus, the animals eat voraciously—with no regard for their well-being or their actual need for food.

That automatic eating is just like addiction. *Repeated use of addictive chemical substances can change the brain at an instinctual level, resulting in behavior that perpetuates use of the substances regardless of what's best for the individual* (**neurobiology of addiction**).

In addiction, obtaining and using addictive substances become programmed into the instinctual brain by repetition and reinforcement (conditioning). Addictive chemicals alter mood by increasing the activity of dopamine in the limbic system's nucleus accumbens, which causes reward (pleasure is a positive reinforcement) and/or relief (escape from unpleasantness is a negative reinforcement). Incidental environmental elements (or cues)—people, places, and things—that are present at the time of a reinforcing behavior (such as the use of an addictive substance) produce no reward or relief on their own. But they may become so associated with the reinforcing behavior in the instinctual brain that they "trigger" the behavior when they are encountered.

This means that when someone pursuing addiction recovery meets a circumstance linked to their addiction, automatic behavior may take them by surprise. A man in his thirties said, "I wasn't thinking about cocaine. I hadn't used for a couple weeks. I was driving to the grocery store and all of a sudden my car turned onto my dealer's street. For a second I thought the dealer had my car under radio control." A man in his forties was in recovery from alcohol dependence for two years when he went to his first Boston Red Sox game since he stopped drinking. He said, "I was inside Fenway Park maybe ten minutes. Before I knew it, I had a sausage dog in one hand and a beer in the other."

To make matters worse, during active addiction, the portion of the cortex at the front of the brain where the person weighs consequences and makes decisions does not do a good job. Too often, obtaining and using more addictive substance takes precedence over natural rewards such as personal safety, family, and citizenship.

Combine the neurobiology of behavior with the neurobiology of addiction and the result could be called the neurobiology of powerlessness. "Powerless" and "powerlessness" are often controversial in discussions of addiction in part because they have been interpreted as a means by which those with addiction avoid responsibility for their behavior. But consider this: People with addiction who stay sober by working with the laws of nature accept that they can't trust their behavior or their thinking, so they pay meticulous attention to avoiding or otherwise managing exposure to addictive substances and the circumstances of their use. This behavior is highly responsible.

In addition to cultivating a realistic mistrust of themselves and taking responsibility for the details of recovery management, people who stay sober by working with the laws of nature cultivate honest self-disclosure. They put themselves in the presence of respectful others and, at a pace that's appropriate for both themselves and the others, share their story and their feelings. This addresses the **neurobiology of recovery**: *Positive interpersonal relationships change the brain and change behavior by integrating emotions with consciousness, which results in the person becoming more resilient and less self-defeating.*

People with addiction who want to stay sober often require individualized interventions such as residential treatment, specialized counseling or therapy, and/or medications that reduce relapse risk or treat physical or mental illness. But the bare essentials of addiction recovery are the two actions described here: consistently avoid addictive substances—***Keep Your Distance!***—and persistently seek support from others—***Ask for Help!*** Neurobiology justifies their importance, and so do the stories of countless individuals with addiction whose recovery efforts went poorly or well depending upon whether the protagonist worked against or with nature.

The two recovery-oriented actions identified here are so relevant and unchanging that I have come to call them **The Two Pillars of Recovery**®.

3. Keep Your Distance!

Ask people engaged in addiction treatment for a single word to describe where they just came from—a word that sums up the experience of active addiction—and they quickly agree on "hell."

Many years ago, someone asked the then famous and now controversial evangelist Billy Sunday, "What must I do to go to hell?" Sunday replied, "Nothing." In other words, make no effort and you will get there. Beliefs about religion and an afterlife aside, Sunday's answer speaks to people who want to get free from active addiction: Make no effort—do what comes naturally—and you will keep returning to hell.

Statistics bear witness to the enormous human and dollar costs of addiction—and some measures keep going up. As a society, if we hope to reduce the toll of addiction, we must recognize not only that addiction can be thought of as a brain disease, but also that addiction persists in individual lives and gets started in additional lives due to *deficiencies in responsibility throughout society*. We can more readily identify opportunities for constructive action if we differentiate three overlapping areas of responsibility: *Recovery is an individual responsibility. Treatment is a professional responsibility. Prevention is a community responsibility.*

Promoting action in these areas may be difficult. Suggest that *someone else* do a better job, and we may be heard as preachy or blaming. Heck, we may *be* preachy or blaming. Blaming makes matters worse. For example, when individuals with addiction are judged, and therefore stigmatized, it becomes more difficult for them to change.

Perhaps all those holding responsibility for addiction can assess *their own* behavior and adjust accordingly. Concerned communities, for example, can make prescription pain medicines less available and their dangers more obvious. Healthcare professionals can become more expert in both human and technical aspects of treating patients with addiction.

What about people living the hell of active addiction? What can they do?

They can—and may have to—do several things. If, for example, they are physically dependent on alcohol, opioids, or sedative-hypnotic medications, they may have to seek medically-managed detoxification to safely discontinue their drug. If their values and lifestyle are centered on drugs, they may have to reorient themselves in a residential program. They may require short- or long-term medication to reduce their risk of resuming substance use or to manage medical or psychiatric illness. Perhaps most important, they must take responsibility for two fundamental actions that work with the laws of nature and that allow recovery to happen. These actions and their underlying neurobiology were described in Section 2 of this *Workbook* and called The Two Pillars of Recovery®. The rest of this Section addresses the first pillar: **Keep Your Distance!**

Addiction changes the brain at an instinctual level. Addictive behavior—seeking and using more of the addictive substance—can occur without regard for the person's well-being and without the person's conscious consent. The decision-making "executive brain" (pre-frontal cortex) may be more strongly attracted to additional substance use than to personal safety and natural rewards such as family or career.

If you have an addictive illness and wish to succeed in recovery—including substance abstinence—you will be wise to cultivate a realistic *mis*trust of yourself and simply not go near addictive substances or circumstances that could prompt their use. For example, you may need to avoid certain people, stores, social gatherings, and holiday rituals. You may need to forsake carrying much cash or a credit card. To remain in recovery, some individuals had to distance themselves from family, romantic partners, or neighborhoods. Some changed careers. Early recovery from addiction is a time to be flexible and practical, not stubborn or proud.

Picture yourself in a motor vehicle, stopped on a steep slope, with the foot brake out of commission. The parking brake is the only mechanism between you and a scary ride—or disaster. Nature works by cause and effect: Gravity and physics can't cut you slack. Neither can neurobiology. If you place yourself too close to addictive substances, or try just one, it's the same as releasing the parking break: Brace yourself for a scary ride—or disaster.

"Eighty percent of success is showing up."
~ Woody Allen

"Just be damn careful where you show up."
~ Geoff Kane

4. *Ask for Help!*

Ever wonder why so many of us lose our voices at the precise moment we need to ask for help? Credit *shame*, the pivotal emotion that drives self-defeating behavior, together with *all-or-nothing thinking*, our most common cognitive distortion.

"Shame," much like "stress," means different things to different people. Here, shame refers to our ongoing sense that we are imperfect. Our sense of an imperfect self can serve us *well*—provided we accept it and are open about it with other human beings. Then it generates empathy and positive interpersonal connections. But all too often shame is toxic. We feel *convinced* we are less than, unworthy, and deserve to be rejected. We may automatically believe that, at all costs, we must not reveal our true selves, fearing that if we do, other people will want nothing to do with us.

We all have a personal burden of shame that is toxic. Shame develops (just as the very structure of the brain develops) through interactions with other people. When people disrespect us—when they communicate disrespect for our person and our limitations through myriad subtle or obvious forms of abuse and neglect, particularly in childhood—the resulting shame pollutes our perceptions of ourselves and impairs our ability to accept ourselves as we are. No one escapes shame because none of us grew up with perfect people around us; no one had perfect parents, siblings, other relatives, teachers, preachers, or friends.

To ask for help is to admit we are less than perfect. All-or-nothing thinking says, "If I am flawed in any way, then I am worthless." Put this distortion together with a germ of healthy self-respect. "Wait a minute! Darn it! I'm *not* worthless!" This leads to, "No way am I going to prove I'm worthless when I'm not! I'd rather die than ask for help!"

Sadly, some people with addiction do die because they don't ask for help. They never learned that: *The way out of shame is through it. Honesty is more important than image. It is more important to be practical than it is to be proud.*

Shame is created by toxic interactions with people. The remedy for shame is nourishing interactions with people. As long as we live, the neuroplasticity of the brain allows even deeply established patterns of feeling and thinking to change in response to experience. If we wish to reduce shame and increase our sense of self-worth, thereby becoming less self-defeating and more adaptive, we must find and then actually engage in nourishing interpersonal relationships.

The first obstacle to engaging in nourishing relationships is finding people who are capable of giving us the respect we deserve and need. Professional help is one option. Mutual help meetings are another—many individuals experience more unconditional acceptance at Alcoholics Anonymous, Narcotics Anonymous, SMART Recovery, LifeRing Secular Recovery, Women for Sobriety, Secular Organizations for Sobriety, or Refuge Recovery than they experienced growing up in their family.

The second obstacle, once we have found respectful others to interact with, is finding our voice. Honest self-disclosure is required. The process may be gradual but, if we are to benefit, we need to open our story and our feelings to these nonjudgmental other people. Interacting with honesty and spontaneity (authenticity) can be difficult for those coming from active addiction. They are used to doing the opposite.

It is tragic that some individuals commit themselves to unhealthy isolation by identifying with roles that cut them off from other people, not realizing that other people are what they need most. They may call themselves a "loner," "not a people person," or a "mountain man." But no matter what they call themselves, stubbornly remaining in these roles makes as much sense as a dried-out plant putting up an umbrella when it's raining.

"...openness is the first step toward recovery... addiction remains a secret because of the overwhelming shame associated with it."
~ David Sheff, Afterword, *Beautiful Boy*

"No man can produce great things who is not thoroughly sincere in dealing with himself."
~ James Russell Lowell

"And it helps to also be thoroughly sincere in dealing with others."
~ Geoff Kane

"The most exhausting thing in life is being insincere."
~ Anne Morrow Lindbergh

5. Falling Dominoes: Or, Why You Can't Have "Just One"

Search the internet or type in "falling dominoes" on YouTube and you will be deluged with opportunities to watch videos, often set to music, of vast numbers of colorful rectangles knocking one another over. These productions are extravagant examples of the original "domino effect." They show domino tiles arranged in both straight lines and intricate patterns, each tile balanced on a narrow end with its rear flat facing the front flat of the next. As long as the distances between the tiles are shorter than their length, once the first domino is toppled, all the rest must fall. Or more accurately, all the rest *usually* fall; once in a while a chain reaction jams, the audience sighs, and the videographer cuts to dominoes that *are* falling.

The middle and last dominoes in these arrangements fall because they are subject to laws of nature. Physics and gravity may not yield the results observers expect every time, but their influence is there. The laws of nature take no time off. People with addiction are also subject to laws of nature. Life sciences show more variation than physical sciences, and outcomes derived from the biology of behavior, psychoactive substances, and the brain are less uniform than outcomes derived from physics and gravity. Nevertheless, behavioral outcomes of some situations are highly predictable. And sadly, lots of well-intentioned people who want to recover from addiction act as though the laws of nature do not apply to them.

Individuals who obtain help for addiction often begin recovery with great enthusiasm. They enjoy time off from alcohol and other addictive substances and restore order in their lives. But then, perhaps touched by complacency, some of them shift away from the programs and people that helped them get sober. To their surprise and indignation, many of these people find themselves not only using addictive substances again, but using out of control. When they say, "I was only going to have one or two" or "I really thought I could control it" they reveal their lack of understanding of the laws of nature that govern addiction and recovery—or their lack of willingness to live in accordance with those laws. Some individuals repeat this many times.

While it goes against the traditional belief that human beings are "rational animals," neuroscience shows that not all human behavior arises from the self-aware cerebral cortex. Rather, much behavior is driven by deeper structures such as the brain stem and limbic system, which are more instinctual or "primitive." Have you ever flirted with someone, for example, before you even realized you were attracted to them? Addictive behavior is driven by these deeper brain structures and can proceed, not only without the consent of the thinking person, but also despite the opposition of the thinking person.

When a person with addiction who has been abstinent takes "just one" of their substance and returns to active addiction, scientists call it "drug-induced reinstatement" of addictive behavior. Researchers have identified some of the nervous system dominoes that bump one another to make this happen. They include the neurotransmitter glutamate and a circuit that connects parts of the brain called ventral pallidum, nucleus accumbens, and medial prefrontal cortex. We might expect the "thinking" part of that circuit, the medial prefrontal cortex, to resist a relapse. Unfortunately, addiction distorts a person's ability to assign values and weigh consequences to such an extent that more substance intake can be the overriding priority.

Creators of domino web videos want lots of dominoes to fall. How long the arrangements stand is not their interest. But do you suppose they ever tip over the first domino and expect nothing else will happen?

"New research shows that emotions have a separate system of nerve pathways, through the limbic system to the cortex, allowing emotional signals to avoid conscious control."

"...unconscious decisions for action go on constantly inside the head."

"We're worse off than Freud thought, because many actions proceed without our knowing anything about them."

~ Robert Ornstein
The Evolution of Consciousness, 1991

6. Sedative-Hypnotic Medications: Nothing to be Relaxed About

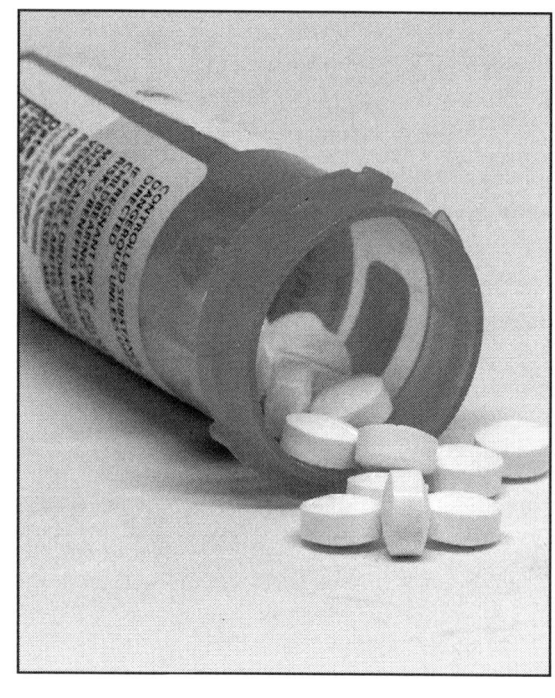

Sedative-hypnotic medications are not good choices for individuals with addiction. Even those without addiction but with increased vulnerability to addiction due to a family history of alcohol dependence, for example, run a higher risk of developing problems with these substances. Nevertheless, some medical practitioners are quick to prescribe sedative-hypnotics when patients complain of anxiety or insomnia. Such prescribers wish to be helpful, but too often these prescriptions end up harming the patient and potentially others.

Though some authors classify sedating antidepressants and antihistamines as sedative-hypnotics, this discussion restricts the category to medications that act in the brain by augmenting the effects of gamma-aminobutyric acid (GABA). GABA is a chemical messenger that inhibits the activity of brain cells. Boosting GABA both calms the brain and increases dopamine in the nucleus accumbens. That increase of dopamine is the neurobiological event most identified with the experience of pleasure and reward. The intensity of the pleasure might be subtle or dramatic. Either way, reward makes the person likely to repeat the experience (taking the medication) that triggered the dopamine surge. Prolonged use of a sedative-hypnotic medication may cause tolerance (people need more to obtain the same effect) and withdrawal (people become ill if they suddenly stop the medication). These pharmacologic actions mean that sedative-hypnotic medications qualify as addictive chemical substances.

Never assume that a medication is safe for you just because a doctor prescribed it. If you are in addiction recovery, actively addicted, or have a family history of alcoholism, it may be all too easy for you to become dependent on a sedative-hypnotic—or for its effects to prime you for a return to your addictive substance of choice. Some individuals in addiction treatment trace the beginning of their addiction, or the beginning of a relapse, back to their use of a benzodiazepine. If you accept the recommendation here to avoid sedative-hypnotics even if you have a willing prescriber, it should go without saying that it is unwise to try one just because a friend or drug dealer thinks it's a good idea.

Medications are not the only remedies for life's problems, though addictive thinking might believe they are. Explore relaxation and other non-pharmacologic treatments if you are troubled by anxiety; sleep hygiene (established guidelines for promoting sleep) if you are troubled by insomnia.

The main objective of this section, however, is not to help you relax or to sleep; it's to help you avoid dangerous medication choices—all the sedative-hypnotics. But please don't let the following information distract you from recovery. Some individuals with addiction strive to obtain information about prescription medications the way some gourmets strive to obtain recipes. For example, copies of the Physicians' Desk Reference, a compendium on prescription medications, have been known to go missing from addiction treatment units. On one unit, a patient in a group discussing the dangers of specific medications was wearing a T-shirt emblazoned "Massachusetts College of Pharmacy."

Sedative-hypnotics are a diverse group. They include not only alcohol, but also medications seldom used today, such as chloral hydrate, meprobamate (Miltown, Equanil), and paraldehyde. Sedative-hypnotics also include medications in the chemical family barbiturates, which are prescribed infrequently now that we have alternatives less likely to cause respiratory depression. Phenobarbital (Luminal, Solfoton), however, is still sometimes employed as an anticonvulsant or to detoxify patients from other sedative-hypnotics such as benzodiazepines or alcohol. Another barbiturate, butalbital, is widely distributed in headache tablets that also contain caffeine and either acetaminophen or aspirin (Fiorinal, Fioricet, Esgic, and others). Variations omit caffeine or add codeine. When the urine of a patient admitted for addiction treatment tests positive for a barbiturate, the most common reason is the presence of butalbital. While prescribers advise patients to take these headache pills sparingly, individuals with addiction have been known to take twenty tablets a day.

The majority of the sedative-hypnotics are in the chemical family benzodiazepines. Chlordiazepoxide (Librium) and diazepam (Valium) were developed first. All benzodiazepines have the same mechanism of action even though they vary in potency, speed of onset, duration of action, and clinical application. Benzodiazepines are the most common agent used to detoxify individuals from alcohol and other sedative-hypnotics. Additional benzodiazepines include: alprazolam (Xanax), clonazepam (Klonopin), clorazepate (Tranxene), estazolam (ProSom, Eurodin), flunitrazepam (Rohypnol), flurazepam (Dalmane), lorazepam (Ativan), midazolam (Versed), oxazepam (Serax), temazepam (Restoril), and triazolam (Halcyon).

The sedative-hypnotic category also encompasses medications some call the Z-drugs, which feature "z" in their generic names: zolpidem (Ambien), zopiclone (Zimovane, Imovane), zaleplon (Sonata), and eszopiclone (Lunesta). The chemical structures of the Z-drugs differ from those of the benzodiazepines, but they act at the same receptor sites in the brain and increase the activity of GABA. Prescribers advise patients who are having trouble sleeping to use zolpidem for brief periods and to take no more than five or 10 milligrams per night; however, individuals with addiction have reported taking 80 to 100 or more milligrams a day for months at a time.

Carisoprodol (Soma) is a sedative-hypnotic prescribed primarily as a muscle relaxant. The liver transforms a significant portion of ingested carisoprodol to meprobamate, which was introduced in the 1950s and was "mother's little helper" until it was superseded by the benzodiazepines a decade later. Problem: Carisoprodol has serious potential for abuse and addiction but American prescribers have been largely unaware of that. Like all sedative-hypnotics, carisoprodol acts like alcohol in the brain. Like benzodiazepines, it has caused overdose deaths and withdrawal seizures. Several European countries removed meprobamate and carisprodol from the market because they considered their risks to outweigh their benefits. In the United States, however, where benzodiazepines have long been regulated as controlled substances, carisoprodol only became classified as a controlled substance in January 2012.

Some individuals with addiction know about carisoprodol's addictive properties and manipulate unsuspecting prescribers to get it. Others discover it by accident. A man is his fifties entered the hospital for treatment of alcohol dependence. In the past he had been given carisoprodol for a muscle problem, and he'd continued to take it. He reported with a smile that he really liked it the first time he took it because it reminded him of alcohol. So, just as with alcohol, he took more and more. He was in treatment several days before he reluctantly agreed to give up this prescribed medication.

Besides reward, rebound can make it difficult for someone to stop a sedative-hypnotic. The pharmacologic rebound effect is when symptoms repeatedly relieved by a medication come back, perhaps stronger than they were originally, when the medication is stopped. Rebound is especially noticeable with short-acting agents, such as alprazolam and lorazepam. Because of rebound, treating anxiety or insomnia with a sedative-hypnotic can be like stopping a swinging pendulum by tapping it with a baseball bat. It works at first; the tap stops the pendulum. But the bat's impact adds energy to the system—so the pendulum swings higher and comes down harder the next time.

Play it safe. If you are troubled by anxiety, insomnia, or muscle spasm, be open-minded about treatments that don't use medications at all. If you do try medication, have your prescriber help you select from options that are not potentially addictive. If you believe nothing will help except one of the substances identified here, be aware that in general the harder you push for a potentially addictive medication, the more likely the push is motivated by addiction and not by medical need.

"Life is painting a picture, not doing a sum."
~ Oliver Wendell Holmes, Jr.

"We are more alike than we are unalike."
~ Maya Angelou
Letter to My Daughter, 2008

7. Recovery: Can You Have It *Your* Way?

People on paths of addiction recovery—and those who dedicate their professional lives to helping others get on such paths—often think of recovery as a spiritual process. These stakeholders might discuss their own sense of spirituality, perhaps referring to relationships and connectedness, and they might engage in practices such as meditation, which many consider spiritual. But they routinely avoid taking positions on how other people ought to understand and practice spirituality. They welcome atheists and agnostics. They consider it up to the individual to decide, for example, whether to incorporate God, prayer, and/or religion into their spiritual lives.

Even though stakeholders who promote recovery encourage people in need of recovery to practice spirituality in whatever non-hurtful ways are meaningful to them, they tend to be less open-minded toward how those same people pursue "recovery." Stakeholders generally have strong, and sometimes conflicting, views on how people emerge from addiction.

Practical wisdom and medical-scientific knowledge about addiction and recovery have been accumulating for decades. The points of view and knowledge bases of persons in recovery and of addiction treatment professionals draw from all that, but what portions of this base individual members of these groups know or consider important differs as well as overlaps. Persons in recovery and treatment professionals debate among themselves how to best define recovery and what to recommend that the willing person do or not do to achieve recovery.

The bone of most contention among participants in these debates seems to be how strictly to interpret the "sobriety" and "abstinence" that most stakeholders agree are essential aspects of recovery. Historically, abstinence has been interpreted in all-or-nothing fashion, which makes it problematic to find a place in recovery for individuals whose abstinence from their drug of choice is inconsistent, or who continue to use tobacco, or whose stability requires medication, especially a medication with addiction or abuse potential such as methadone or buprenorphine. "Harm reduction" connotes clinical and social achievement to some, but distasteful compromise to others. Concepts such as "partial recovery," "recover*ing* vs. in recovery," and "addiction as a chronic disease with varying durations of remission" have been proposed but not widely adopted.

Can we find a more unifying way to think about addiction and recovery? A framework that respects the diversity of those affected, yet also respects the laws of nature that govern addiction and recovery? We know enough about the nature—the neurobiology—of addiction and of recovery to know that people seeking recovery do better when they work *with* nature by avoiding addictive substances and cultivating positive interpersonal relationships. Those who resist nature by ignoring those two actions tend to stay stuck in addiction—and judge themselves harshly for their lack of progress. They strive to fix things on their own, without realizing that what works in nature is not arbitrary.

We might, for example, imagine each willing person as getting on a path of recovery, equipped as necessary with tools such as medication or residential treatment to provide traction and support on their journey. They will be more likely to make progress on that journey with our acceptance and encouragement, and perhaps with gentle reminders to take action—after all, they are on a path, not a moving sidewalk. Can we respect variability and honor persistence?

"Addiction is like gravity— governed by laws of nature that never take time off."
~ Geoff Kane

"There is more to who we are and more to why we do the things we do than what meets our own minds... Lower centers of the Central Nervous System can, and routinely do, act independently of higher centers."
~ Geoff Kane

"...we cannot save our face and our ass at the same time."
~ *Narcotics Anonymous* (4th Edition, p 78)

8. It All Comes Down to Your Choices

"It all comes down to your choices," said a man in his fifties as he completed the treatment that interrupted his brief return to drinking lots of alcohol. For three weeks, in the company of supportive peers and an empathic treatment team, this man had immersed himself in mindfulness practices structured by Acceptance and Commitment Therapy (ACT). He also maintained connections with his sponsor and Alcoholics Anonymous. The man recounted how an offer of alcohol—made amid physical, interpersonal, and financial stressors—precipitated his most recent drinking episode. Similar situations had instigated previous binges.

In the future, he plans to minimize exposure to stressors and to drinking opportunities. When stressors or alcohol are unavoidable, he anticipates choosing to notice them without reacting in ways that conflict with his values. "Personal responsibility" for "choices" protects his paramount value, sobriety. Such clarity is too rare. Many others with addiction—and people around them—would do well to adopt this perspective. Choices represent the way out of active addiction, much as they represent the way in.

It's confusing because conscious choices made by individuals in active addiction often don't matter. Addiction is compulsive—people in addiction frequently behave opposite to their own wishes and values. Science explains that addictive behavior is driven by the primitive region of the brain that does not reliably respond to intentions or conscious decisions. Even though people in addiction may repeatedly declare they value self-preservation, family, and community, their behavior suggests they do not.

Addictive substance use—and the self-destructive and relationship-damaging consequences that typically accompany it—generates anger and frustration in both bystanders and the person using. This occurs largely because people often assume that the substance use is a chosen behavior. For example, individuals with addiction berate themselves when they choose to stop using but don't. And people around them berate them not only for not stopping but also because they frequently do not seem to take responsibility for the harm brought about by their apparent choices.

It's helpful to understand that human behavior may be either chosen or determined (unaffected by choice). It can also be a blend of the two. Chosen behaviors are often guided by values and preferences (like selecting music). Determined behaviors are often driven by instinct (like gasping for air when you can no longer hold your breath) or by unrecognized feelings (like intending to be funny, not recognizing anger, and coming out with sarcasm). As for a blend, how many of our good deeds are motivated by a conscious desire to serve others *and* by an unconscious desire for approval?

In addiction, the urge to obtain and consume more substance is strong and irrational, like the urge to survive or reproduce. A man in his twenties, addicted to opioids, said, "I use like my life depends on it."

Timing, values, and accountability

Choices to exit active addiction—or not enter addiction at all—are much more likely to matter if they are made before or after the person is consumed with seeking and using more substance. The man described at the beginning of this section, who recognizes and accepts his personal responsibility to avoid drinking, reached his conclusions only after friends brought him to a hospital for alcohol detoxification and further treatment.

It can be difficult for young people who prefer not to overdose or become addicted to make choices that protect those values. They may, for example, be vulnerable to addiction due to genetics and adverse childhood experiences, obtain addictive substances easily, and hang out with peers who glorify substance use. A blog article on the dangers of synthetic marijuana and salvia attracted young readers because the title—"How to Blow Your Mind"—appeared to offer new ways to get high.

Many individuals now in addiction recovery learned to take more responsibility for their choices when they "hit bottom" and realized it would be more painful to stay the same than to change. We make it less comfortable to stay the same when we respectfully hold those in addiction accountable for their behavior. They don't have to enjoy the process—drug courts work even when people in them don't want to be there.

One clinician reminds others of responsibility and consequences/accountability with this plaque: "Have a nice day, unless you've made other plans."

"Happiness cannot be sought directly; it is a by-product of love and service."
~ *Twenty-Four Hours a Day*

"May your inherent knowing guide you."
~ Marta Carbone

9. Workbook: My Commitments

This booklet describes two actions nature requires of people with addiction if they want to stay sober. The actions are validated by hard-won practical wisdom and the latest brain science.

If you are actively addicted to a chemical substance—whether it's alcohol, an addictive medication, or a street drug—and you desire the safety, balance, and satisfaction of addiction recovery, then get busy. People can't recover from addiction without taking action any more than they can get physically fit without moving their bodies.

You will be more likely to remember and keep your commitments if you write them down. Organize your notes in the pages that follow under the two pillars of recovery: ***Keep Your Distance!*** and ***Ask for Help!***

As you record your responses, keep in mind that alcohol is a drug. Enter your first name in the spaces provided. If you are new to recovery, you may want to look over these questions and your answers every morning until abstinence becomes your way of life.

In the **Recovery Journal**, write whatever you please. It can be easier to explore your feelings if you write quickly and don't worry about grammar or punctuation. If you are right-handed, try writing with your left hand to reach deeper feelings (lefties do the opposite). It's up to you whether or not you share what you write.

You are welcome to make photocopies of the four Workbook pages for your own use or to share with others. These pages may also be dowloaded from geoffkane.com.

"A feeling of self-respect flows into us when we stand up and say 'I did something wrong.' This statement also says, 'I have the strength to face my responsibilities and repair my mistakes.' It is surprisingly helpful to our self-esteem, and it improves our relationships."
~ M. A. F.
Touchstones, 1986, 1991

The Two Pillars of Recovery® Workbook   Geoff Kane, MD, MPH

Keep Your Distance!

I, _____, will avoid or protect myself from addictive substances and the circumstances of their use. I will not consume substance(s) out of addiction. I will not even be near them without reliable support.

Fill in the blanks as specifically as possible—list brands; first names of people; names of towns, businesses, etc.

My first choice drug(s) / substance(s) _____

My favorite substitute substance if my first choice is not available _____

Other substances I must watch out for _____

Harm that my use of those substances has already caused to my:

    relationships _____

    school or work _____

    finances _____

    body _____

My main excuses (justifications, rationalizations) to myself and others for why it is okay for me to continue to use drugs despite the harm _____
_____
_____

Where I usually obtain drug(s) _____

People who help me get drugs _____

How I pay for drugs _____

Where I consume them _____

Who I consume them with _____

Time(s) of day _____

Activities related to my use of drugs (*cooking, cookouts, concerts, clubs, sports, after work, dancing, sex…*)
_____
_____
_____

Occasions when it's especially hard not to use (*weekends, paydays, holidays, birthdays, weddings…*)
_____
_____

The Two Pillars of Recovery® Workbook   Geoff Kane, MD, MPH

Things I better not touch or even see (*pipes, roach clips, lighters, special glassware, needles...*) _____
_____
_____
_____

Items and situations I must avoid or have help to carefully manage (*cash, credit cards, access to car or truck, internet access, airplane or other travel...*) _____
_____
_____
_____

Relationships I associate with drug use (*Are you more likely to use when the relationship is going well or not going well?*) _____
_____
_____
_____

Memories I associate with drug use (*especially memories you avoid by using*) _____
_____
_____
_____

Feelings I associate with drug use (*especially feelings you avoid by using*) _____
_____
_____
_____

Other matters I must address to protect my recovery _____
_____
_____
_____
_____
_____

Signed _____ *Date* _____

Ask for Help!

I, _____, will honestly share my story—especially my mistakes and my feelings—with a respectful other person or group in order to build resilience and my ability to cope in all areas of my life including my recovery. I will identify people appropriate to my needs and ask for their help.

Fill in the blanks as specifically as possible—list family members, friends, professionals, peers in recovery, etc. Use first names except for professionals.

When I want to use drug(s) or go near them, before I start, I will call _____
_____

If I can't reach her/him, I will call _____

Or _____

If I see them at all, I will ask these people (whom I associate with obtaining or using drugs) to leave me alone, and I will be rude if necessary _____
_____
_____

If I must go where I will have access to substances (such as alcohol at the supermarket or prescription medication at the doctor's office), I will ask one of the following people who support my recovery to go with me
_____
_____
_____

Places where I can meet sober people _____
_____
_____

People to share healthful activities _____
_____
_____

People to help me through times when it's especially hard not to use _____
_____
_____

The Two Pillars of Recovery® Workbook   Geoff Kane, MD, MPH

People to help me get rid of all my drug-related paraphernalia _____
_____
_____

People to help me manage cash, credit, and transportation _____
_____
_____

People to talk with about relationships _____
_____

About memories _____
_____

About feelings _____
_____

How I will seek help from the Universe / Higher Power of my understanding (*specify at least one daily spiritual practice such as yoga, meditation, or inspirational reading*) _____
_____
_____

Other help I will need for recovery _____
_____
_____
_____
_____
_____
_____
_____

Signed _____ *Date* _____

Recovery Journal

Recovery Journal

Recovery Journal

Recovery Journal

Recovery Journal

Recovery Journal

Recovery Journal

Made in the USA
Middletown, DE
16 September 2025

13495030R00022